ETERNITY IS NOW IN SESSION

PARTICIPANT's
GUIDE

ETERNITY
IS NOW
IN SESSION

A RADICA   HAT JESUS

REALL   ATION,

ETERNITY, A   OOD PLACE

PARTICIPANT'S GUIDE

JOHN
ORTBERG
& GARY MOON

TYNDALE
MOMENTUM®

The nonfiction imprint of
Tyndale House Publishers, Inc.

Visit Tyndale online at www.tyndale.com.

Visit Tyndale Momentum online at www.tyndalemomentum.com.

TYNDALE, Tyndale Momentum, and Tyndale's quill logo are registered trademarks of Tyndale House Publishers, Inc. The Tyndale Momentum logo is a trademark of Tyndale House Publishers, Inc. Tyndale Momentum is the nonfiction imprint of Tyndale House Publishers, Inc., Carol Stream, Illinois.

For information about special discounts for bulk purchases, please contact Tyndale House Publishers at csresponse@tyndale.com, or call 1-800-323-9400.

ISBN 978-1-4964-3169-1

Printed in the United States of America

24	23	22	21	20	19	18
7	6	5	4	3	2	1

CONTENTS

INTRODUCTION

Thank you for choosing to use *Eternity Is Now in Session* for your group. This participant's guide is designed to accompany the *Eternity Is Now in Session DVD Experience* and the book *Eternity Is Now in Session* by John Ortberg. This study guide is five sessions long and will help participants grow closer to God as they rediscover "what Jesus really taught about salvation, eternity, and getting to the good place." The sessions will show participants what it means to follow Jesus in discipleship through the stages of awakening, purgation, illumination, and union.

Each session follows a similar format: there is a video with teaching from John Ortberg, discussion questions for group reflection, and a key activity that invites participants to go deeper into the topic studied. There are also suggestions for ways that participants can engage this study throughout the week (including reading corresponding chapters in the book *Eternity Is Now in Session*) and Scripture passages that follow the theme of the session.

Your group should have a leader who is responsible for

starting the video, prompting participants with the discussion questions, and directing the key activity. The leader should also monitor the time and can adjust the session's activities and discussion accordingly. (See "Leader Tips" on page xi.)

John writes, "God is not waiting for eternity to begin. God lives in it right now. It is the interactive fellowship and joy that exists between Father, Son, and Holy Spirit. Eternity is rolling right along, and we are invited to be part of it—*now*." Are you ready to join in?

Eternity is now in session!

MATERIALS NEEDED

This *Eternity Is Now in Session Participant's Guide* is intended to accompany the *Eternity Is Now in Session DVD Experience* and the *Eternity Is Now in Session* book. Each session of this curriculum is intended to last sixty to ninety minutes. In order to get the most out of this study, we recommend that you have the following materials present at your meetings:

- One copy of the *Eternity Is Now in Session DVD Experience* for the group
- A copy of the *Eternity Is Now in Session* book and this participant's guide for each person
- A DVD player and TV or a computer (to watch the video component for each session)
- A clock (to monitor time)
- A pen or pencil for each person (to take notes during the video and for use in each session's key activity)
- A Bible for each person

LEADER TIPS

The following are some tips that will help you as you lead your group through the *Eternity Is Now in Session* study:

BEFORE THE SESSION

- Watch the video (if possible) and look over the study notes, discussion questions, and activities in the participant's guide in advance of the meeting.
- Pray by name for each person who will be at the session and ask that God would open new avenues for intimacy with this person through the study.
- Consider preparing (or appointing someone to prepare) a snack for the session. Snacks can loosen an atmosphere and make people more comfortable with sharing.
- Make sure the materials needed (page ix) are present at every session. It's a good idea to arrive early in case of problems.
- Encourage study participants to read the chapters in *Eternity Is Now in Session* in advance of your meetings. While reading the chapters isn't necessary to use the

participant's guide or DVD, participants will get the most out of the experience by following along in the book.

AT THE SESSION

- Be sure to welcome each person to the group when they arrive, and carry that spirit of welcome throughout the session.
- Try to encourage each person to speak during the discussion.
- Don't be afraid to adapt the material provided in this study—cutting questions or lingering on a topic—to provide the best experience for your group.
- Be mindful of participants' time, and do your best to keep the study within the parameters you've set for the group. That being said, if the Holy Spirit is moving, do what you can to allow extra time and space to minister.
- Remind participants of the homework activities that accompany each session, which can be accomplished throughout the week. Highlight one or more of these activities and request reports at your next session.
- Consider taking prayer requests at the close of your session or breaking into smaller groups for prayer.

Session 1

ARE WE THERE YET?

WELCOME

Welcome to session 1 of the *Eternity Is Now in Session DVD Experience*. Each of the five sessions in this study is designed to be completed in 60 to 90 minutes, with additional activities that you can do at home.

This session accompanies chapters 1–3 of the *Eternity Is Now in Session* book (pages 11–63). Watch the video, discuss the questions, and complete the key activity as a group as time allows.

VIDEO NOTES

As you watch the video, use the space below to take notes. We've included some key points to get you started.

Jesus—and the entire New Testament, for that matter—defines eternal life only once, with great precision, and in a way that has been largely lost in our day.

> This is eternal life, that they may know you, the only true God, and Jesus Christ whom you have sent.
>
> JOHN 17:3, NRSV

To know God means to know what Paul called "the power of his resurrection" (Philippians 3:10) in the details and tasks and challenges of my daily, ordinary life.

God is not waiting for eternity to begin. God lives in it right now. Eternity is now in session.

> The New Testament is a book about disciples,
> by disciples, and for disciples of Jesus Christ.
>
> DALLAS WILLARD

Discipleship is a journey—a lifelong journey in which we learn to live the life that Jesus offers. For many centuries, that journey was described using certain stages:

- **Awakening:** I become aware of God's extraordinary presence in my ordinary days. I wake up to love, gratitude, wonder, and responsibility.
- **Purgation:** I confess my character defects. I humbly ask God to remove them. I engage in practices that can help free me from them.
- **Illumination:** I begin to change at the level of my automatic perceptions and beliefs. My "mental map" of how things are begins to look like Jesus' mental map.
- **Union:** I begin to experience the life that Jesus invited us into when he said, "Abide in me, and I will abide in you" (see John 15:4).

DISCUSSION QUESTIONS

1. In John 17:3 Jesus defines eternal life as *knowing* God. What does it mean to know God? How does this differ from knowing *about* God?

2. What is the significance of eternity being in session right now?

3. What are any barriers you may have to experiencing Jesus as your "shepherd" or "your very good friend" as you go through each day? Why are these things in the way?

4. How would you define *discipleship* to a friend?

5. Without looking at the notes above, how many movements from John's description of the journey of discipleship can you name? Which do you think best characterizes your walk with Jesus now? Explain.

6. How would you live differently if it were organized around living in an interactive relationship with the Trinity? What specifically would change?

KEY ACTIVITY: KNOWING GOD

BELIEF VS. KNOWLEDGE

Belief and *knowledge* are two very different words. We can believe something even if it is false. We can believe, for example, that the moon is made of cheese or that the universe sprang from nothingness without assistance. Jesus knew that even the demons in hell believed he was the Son of God. But, as Dallas Willard has written, "We have knowledge of something when we are representing it (thinking about it, speaking of it, treating it) as it actually is, on an appropriate basis of thought and experience."[1] Knowledge is truth based on adequate evidence.

So when John states that "eternal life = knowing God," he is talking about stepping into a belief. We can believe that a chair can support our bodies. We know this is true when we trust the chair with our weight. Eternal living means trusting our lives to what is real, present, and right here. Knowledge takes belief to a new and experiential level.

- If knowing God through living *with* the Trinity is the key to understanding who we are, and why we are here, what are some practical ways you can live more moments of your life "with" God?

---

[1] Dallas Willard. *Knowing Christ Today: Why We Can Trust Spiritual Knowledge* (New York: HarperOne, 2009), 15.

DISCERNING GOD'S VOICE

As you live in more active conversation with your good friend Jesus, you may want to consider the following questions to help you recognize the voice of God.

1. **Does it sound like God?** Does what you heard sound like something God would say? Is it consistent with God as you know him through Scripture?

2. **Does it sound like Jesus Christ?** Does it sound like something Jesus would say? Is it consistent with Jesus as you see him revealed in the pages of the New Testament?

3. **Does it help you be conformed to the image of Christ?** The glory of God is our transformation into Christlikeness (see 2 Corinthians 3:18).

4. **Is it consistent with a previous experience you have had that you now know was from God?** We can take advantage of the 20/20 vision of hindsight.

5. **Is it consistent with the fruit of the Spirit, and does it promote the growth of Christ's character in us?** The fruit of the Spirit is the character of Christ.

6. **Is it consistent with the witness of what the saints and devotion masters have had to say about God?** Do I get a witness from those who have won the race?

7. **Do my closest friends and spiritual mentors believe it was from God?** Do I get a witness from those I trust?

8. **Is it consistent with the overarching themes of Scripture?** God's spoken word will not contradict his written Word.

What questions would you add to this list?

HOMEWORK: RECOGNIZE AND RESPOND

Before the next session, read chapter 4, "Awakening" (pages 75–98), in the *Eternity Is Now in Session* book. Consider also completing the following activity:

FRANK LAUBACH AND THE "GAME WITH MINUTES"

Frank Laubach is a great example of a person who got to know God and lived his life very differently based on that knowledge.[2]

---

[2] This discussion of Frank Laubach is adapted from Gary Moon, *Falling for God: Saying Yes to His Extravagant Proposal* (Colorado Springs: WaterBrook, 2004), 89–92. Used by permission of the publisher.

On March 23, 1930, Laubach wrote in his diary, "Can we have contact with God all the time? All the time awake, fall asleep in his arms, and awaken in His presence, can we attain that? Can we do His will all the time? Can we think His thoughts all the time?"

When he posed these questions, forty-five-year-old Laubach was laboring under a cloud of profound dissatisfaction, despite his academic achievements—a BA from Princeton, a graduate degree from Union Theological Seminary, and an MA and PhD in sociology from Columbia University—and his success as a missionary to the Philippines. For fifteen years he had won praise as a teacher, writer, and administrator.

Laubach's sterling achievements make it doubly puzzling when we read the self-assessment he made at the halftime of his life: "As for me, I never lived, I was half dead; I was a rotting tree."

Even as his churches filled with converts, his heart was becoming crowded with loneliness, discouragement, and mild depression. Even after planting a seminary in the Philippines to train missionaries, he confessed that he had learned nothing of surrender and joy in Christ.

How can that be? Frank Laubach spoke of God daily. He had a devoted wife and family and all the trappings of success. Why was he so weighed down with doubt and despair?

Like Augustine's, Laubach's soul would forever feel restless and alone until nestled into the arms of God; it would forever feel lonely until awake to constant companionship with God. He was waiting for something more.

Laubach determined to do something about his miserable

condition and decided to make the rest of his life a continuous inner conversation with God, in perfect responsiveness to God's will so that his own life could become rich with God's presence.

All he could do was throw himself open to God. All he could do was raise the windows and unlock the doors of his soul. But he also knew that these simple acts of the will were very important and so he resolved to spend as many moments as possible in listening and determined sensitivity to God's presence.

He invented something he called a "game with minutes." Laubach's "game" is a method of calling God to mind at least one second of each minute for the purpose of awareness and conversation.

As he began to live moment by moment in attentiveness to God's presence, Laubach experienced a remarkable change. By the end of the first month of his experiment with the game, he had gained a sense of being carried along by God through the hours of cooperation with him in little things.

When Laubach began his experiment he was living among the fierce Moros, an anti-Christian, Islamic tribe on Mindanao. Not long after he began to keep constant company with God, the Moros began to notice the difference. Two of the leading Muslim leaders began telling people that Laubach could help them know God. And even though he never pretended to be anything other than a follower of Jesus, the Moros began to take Laubach into their hearts and lives, loving, trusting, and helping him without regard to their cultural and religious differences.

Laubach lived the second half of his life as God's constant companion. His life is a picture of the path of real change. He took the *time* to be with God, was *honest* about the condition of his heart, and trusted that God *desired* the same intimate relationship that he craved.

GAME WITH MINUTES IDEAS

Make a list of some ways you might become more aware of God's presence as you go through your day. We'll start you with a few ideas from Laubach's "game with minutes."

1. Wake up and greet God with a warm "good morning" and listen for his response.

2. Read favorite portions of Scripture as faded love letters— listening for the voice of the Author as you read.

3. Recognize the long line at the grocery store as an opportunity for a few deep breaths and a time to listen for the voice of God.

4. Make sure your day planner has at least one appointment with God that is written in indelible ink. Close the door. Offer him an empty chair. Then be quiet, be patient, and lean in.

5. See each person you meet as a new opportunity to show love to the *imago dei* (the image of God inside them). God's reflection is on every face.

6. Make hugging your close family or friends a sacrament of communicating love to God.

7. When you turn the light out, ask God if he enjoyed spending the day together and listen for his response.

SCRIPTURE FOR REFLECTION

The following passages of Scripture focus on *knowing* God.

> This is eternal life, that they may know you, the only true God, and Jesus Christ whom you have sent.
> JOHN 17:3, NRSV

> We proclaim to you the one who existed from the beginning, whom we have heard and seen. We saw him with our own eyes and touched him with our own hands. He is the Word of life. This one who is life itself was revealed to us, and we have seen him. And now we testify and proclaim to you that he is the one who is eternal life. He was with the Father, and then he was revealed to us. We proclaim to you what we ourselves have actually seen and heard so that you may have fellowship with us. And our fellowship is with the Father and with his Son, Jesus Christ. We are writing these things so that you may fully share our joy.
>
> This is the message we heard from Jesus and now declare to you: God is light, and there is no darkness in him at all.
> 1 JOHN 1:1-5, NLT

> We know that we have come to know him if we keep his commands.
> 1 JOHN 2:3

Dear friends, let us love one another, for love comes from God. Everyone who loves has been born of God and knows God. Whoever does not love does not know God, because God is love. . . . This is how we know that we live in him and he in us: He has given us of his Spirit.

1 JOHN 4:7-8, 13

I want to know Christ—yes, to know the power of his resurrection and participation in his sufferings, becoming like him in his death.

PHILIPPIANS 3:10

That is why I am suffering as I am. Yet this is no cause for shame, because I know whom I have believed, and am convinced that he is able to guard what I have entrusted to him until that day.

2 TIMOTHY 1:12

His divine power has given us everything needed for life and godliness, through the knowledge of him who called us by his own glory and goodness. Thus he has given us, through these things, his precious and very great promises, so that through them you may escape from the corruption that is in the world because of lust, and may become participants of the divine nature.

2 PETER 1:3-4, NRSV

Session 2

AWAKENING

WELCOME

Welcome to session 2 of the *Eternity Is Now in Session DVD Experience*. Each of the five sessions in this study is designed to be completed in 60 to 90 minutes, with additional activities that you can do at home.

This session accompanies chapter 4 of the *Eternity Is Now in Session* book (pages 75–98). Watch the video, discuss the questions, and complete the key activity as a group as time allows.

VIDEO NOTES

As you watch the video, use the space below to take notes. We've included some key points to get you started.

Immanuel means "God with us." God wants to have an intimate relationship with us.

"What Jesus wants—what God wants—is for your home, your school, your office, your neighborhood, your Starbucks to become 'holy land,' because it becomes the place where you and Jesus walk together."

For Jesus to be *with* his apprentices meant he was to become their intimate friend, humble and transparent.

> When they saw the courage of Peter and John and realized that they were unschooled, ordinary men, they were astonished and they took note that these men had been with Jesus.
>
> ACTS 4:13

Dallas Willard said that life is mostly made up of experiences. That is why we treasure them so much. Intimacy is shared experience. Every time we invite God into our lives, we are sharing experiences and increasing intimacy. To love someone means that you are interested in her or his experiences.

> When Jacob awoke from his sleep, he thought,
> "Surely the LORD is in this place,
> and I was not aware of it."
>
> GENESIS 28:16

Jesus said, "You are the light of the world. . . . Let your light shine before others, that they may see your good deeds and glorify your Father in heaven" (Matthew 5:14-16).

It takes two things to experience greater intimacy with God: time and honesty.

DISCUSSION QUESTIONS

1. How can you make your home, office, or Starbucks "holy land"? What has worked for you?

2. Dallas Willard said that persons are mostly made up of experiences. Intimacy is shared experience. What are some ways we can learn more about what God experiences? What are some ways God can learn more about your experiences? What does it look like to share experience with God?

3. What does it look like to listen to Jesus? When should we listen? Where should we listen? How should we listen?

4. In the video, John says that it takes time and honesty to live a life of more intimacy with God. Do you agree? Why or why not? How essential are time and honesty in human relationships?

5. What does it mean that "when you come before the real God and you bring the real self . . . and you're in the presence of Jesus, someday you're gonna glow"? Have you ever known someone so radiant with the love of God that they "glow"? If so, what qualities seemed to make that person glow? What might "glowing" like Jesus look like?

KEY ACTIVITY: UP THE MOUNTAIN / DOWN THE MOUNTAIN—IN EVERYDAY LIFE

As John beautifully describes, Jesus' three closest friends accompanied him up the mountain to see who he and his Father truly are. This reached a crescendo as they fell to the earth—perhaps symbolic of their death to old ways of thinking. And then they got up, resurrected so to speak, into a new way of living and followed Jesus down the mountain, back into everyday life.

Perhaps for Christians each day should include a rhythm of going "up the mountain" to sit in the radiance of God's identity and then going "down the mountain" to live more and more moments of each day in awareness of God's presence.

Take some time to brainstorm ideas for going up and down the mountain with God each day.

UP THE MOUNTAIN IDEAS

Things that will help you to have a sense of soaking in God's presence. (Hint: most ideas will involve either time or honesty.) Here are some ideas to get you started:

- Put fifteen minutes into your calendar each day for sitting with God.
- Listen to a song that causes you to feel lost in God's presence while spending this time with God.
- Memorize a few verses of Scripture that speak of God's desire to be with you.
- Read Bible verses that record the things Jesus did and said.
- Be real and transparent with God—no more hiding; just you coming before God exactly as you are.

DOWN THE MOUNTAIN IDEAS

Things that will help you to live more moments each day with God:

- Rename your alarm clock a "resurrection" clock.
- Before getting out of bed, invite God to go through the day with you.
- Imagine that Jesus is standing beside you when you greet people.
- Thank God for what you are eating, not only before you eat but constantly during the meal.
- Change the way you commute to work, giving thanks for the miracle of transportation and the time your commute provides for honest conversation with God about your day.
- Invite Jesus to sit beside you as you work.
- Invite the Trinity into your problems and ask for ideas.
- Have a conversation with God about your day as the last thing you do before going to sleep.

HOMEWORK: RECOGNIZE AND RESPOND

Before the next session, read chapter 5, "Purgation" (pages 99–124) in the *Eternity Is Now in Session* book. Consider also completing the following activities:

1. WHAT IS YOUR VISION FOR YOUR LIFE WITH GOD?

Write out a page or so on your vision for what your life would be like if transformed by God so that you are living more and more moments aware of his presence and as his intimate friend. Note: The sign of an adequate vision is that it releases your deepest desire.

2. REFLECTION ON FRIENDSHIP

Reflect on the best friendships you have had throughout your life and compare them to your relationship with God. What is the impact of this exercise on your desire for intimacy with God?

3. CHILD OF LIGHT EXERCISE

Rate yourself on how each of the components of you are progressing in their own transfiguration. We'll use what Dallas Willard had to say about a person becoming a "child of light."

- *Thoughts*: Children of light think constantly about God, dwelling upon his greatness and loveliness.
- *Feelings*: Love is the dominant emotion of children of light.
- *Will (spirit, heart)*: They are habitually devoted to doing what is good and right. The will is habitually attuned to surrender and obey.

- *Body*: Their body is constantly poised to do what is right and good.
- *Social Relations*: Children of light are completely transparent in their relations with others.
- *Soul*: All of the above is not just at the surface; these things are deep and effortless.

4. RECOGNIZE AND RESPOND

Ignatius of Loyola, the founder of the Society of Jesus, observed that the best way we can live is in a constant state of recognizing and responding to God's presence with us in all of the mundane and glorious moments of the day. Take a moment to reread the outline, questions, and exercises above and construct a list of things you can do each day to help you recognize and respond to the astounding gift of God's friendship.

SCRIPTURE FOR REFLECTION

You are my friends if you do what I command. I no
longer call you servants, because a servant does not
know his master's business. Instead, I have called you
friends, for everything that I learned from my Father
I have made known to you.

JOHN 15:14-15

Was not our father Abraham considered righteous
for what he did when he offered his son Isaac on
the altar? You see that his faith and his actions were
working together, and his faith was made complete by
what he did. And the scripture was fulfilled that says,
"Abraham believed God, and it was credited to him as
righteousness," and he was called God's friend.

JAMES 2:21-23

Session 3

PURGATION

WELCOME

Welcome to session 3 of the *Eternity Is Now in Session DVD Experience*. Each of the five sessions in this study is designed to be completed in 60 to 90 minutes, with additional activities that you can do at home.

This session accompanies chapter 5 of the *Eternity Is Now in Session* book (pages 99–124). Watch the video, discuss the questions, and complete the key activity as a group as time allows.

VIDEO NOTES

As you watch the video, use the space below to take notes. We've included some key points to get you started.

Jesus begins teaching from the Word of God. He loves people, so he's giving them wisdom about how to live. The people are so hungry for these words that Jesus has to finish his talk from a boat. He sits down and continues teaching.

> Simon answered, "Master, we've worked hard all night and haven't caught anything. But because you say so, I will let down the nets."
>
> LUKE 5:5

Peter doesn't see what Jesus sees, but he is willing to do what Jesus says; that is enough to be a disciple, to be part of a "because you say so" community.

> When Simon Peter saw this, he fell at
> Jesus' knees and said, "Go away from me, Lord;
> I am a sinful man!"
>
> LUKE 5:8

Peter sees Jesus' full identity, and he becomes fully aware of his own identity as being separate and apart from Jesus—a sinner. He becomes aware of his own sinfulness and brokenness.

We are all in the same situation as Peter. We are on the same boat, but it can be the Jesus boat. Church is to be a place for messed-up people, a hospital for souls. Nobody's perfect, but everyone is welcome and nothing is impossible with Jesus.

DISCUSSION QUESTIONS

1. What do you most identify with in this story about a lake, a man, and a boat? Why does this part of the story speak to you?

2. What are some of the barriers you face to becoming a habitual "because you say so" type of Christ follower? What causes these barriers? How might you overcome them?

3. Have you ever had an experience with another person where you expected condemnation but instead received unexpected love? What was your reaction?

4. What do the words *repentance* and *confession* mean? What do you think of when you hear these words? Why are they important to our own spiritual healing?

5. If you were to call 1-800-GOT-JUNK, what is some of the spiritual junk that you might ask to be hauled off? How would this affect your intimacy with God?

KEY ACTIVITY: MOVING TOWARD OR AWAY FROM GOD

James Martin, SJ, in his book *The Jesuit Guide to (Almost) Everything: A Spirituality for Real Life*, presents a modification of Ignatius of Loyola's classic exercise the examen, which is a review of the day. What follows is a slight modification of Martin's modification.[3]

THE EXAMEN IN FIVE STEPS

This prayer can be practiced at any set time of the day, but many enjoy using it in the evening, just before going to bed, as a way of reviewing the day. It is good to remind yourself both that you are in the presence of God and that the aim of this examination is to become progressively more aware of that presence and available friendship as you go through each day. Walk through these five steps as a group.

1. *Gratitude*: Recall events from your day that made you smile with gratefulness. Enjoy the memory, and then breathe a "thanks" to God.

2. *Review*: Recall events from the day where you felt most aware of God's presence and the desire to move toward and with him.

3. *Sorrow*: Recall times during the day when you felt distracted from God's presence and intimacy, times when you felt you were away from God and running your life on your own.

---

3 See James Martin, *The Jesuit Guide to (Almost) Everything: A Spirituality for Real Life* (New York: HarperCollins, 2010), 97.

4. *Forgiveness*: Like Peter at Jesus' feet, humbly ask God to forgive your times of distraction from his presence, especially if during those times you may have caused hurt to anyone, including yourself.

5. *Grace*: Ask God for the grace you need to live more moments tomorrow with the ability to feel the reality of God's presence and love more clearly.

HOMEWORK: RECOGNIZE AND RESPOND

Before the next session, read chapter 6, "Illumination" (pages 125–145), in the *Eternity Is Now in Session* book. Consider also completing the following activities:

1. DAILY EXAMEN

Resolve to set aside time each day to walk through the five steps of the examen as presented above.

2. 1-800-GOT-JUNK

John reminds us that our goal of living more and more moments pursuing intimacy with God (shared experience) takes effort. There are consistent barriers that get in the way of our intimacy with God. Both two thousand years ago and today, there are the same number of hours in the day and a very similar list of distractions from living in awareness of God's presence. Very common barriers are busyness, fear, ambition, guilt, shame, and the consequential tendency to be distracted from the reality of divine presence and love and to move away from instead of toward God. Two thousand years ago and today, we need the same things to overcome the barriers to healing friendship: deep self-awareness, confession, and ongoing examination and repentance.

Take a few minutes and write out your schedule for a typical weekday. What activities are you most likely to be engaged in?

Now, go back over the events of a typical day and label each with either "MT" (activities that are helping you *move toward* God, becoming more aware of divine presence and love) or "MA" (activities that are causing you to *move away* from God, being less aware of divine presence and love).

Use this schedule and talk to God about how you might redeem your time.

3. CONFESSION WITH A PSALM

Read Psalm 51 (see pages 39–41) as a confession to God at least one time this week.

4. CONFESSION WITH AN EMPTY CHAIR

During one of Dallas Willard's last public appearances he said, "Sin always splits the self to some degree, yes. You know that you have harmed yourself and others, but you probably are not going to come to terms with that because you're carrying on a charade of righteousness, even if you don't believe it. So confession is very deep in the process of discovering the soul."[4]

There are several things necessary for giving a good confession: 1) an examination of conscience: inviting God to show us when we are moving away from his Kingdom and into the kingdom of our ego and self-will; 2) sorrow: like Peter, falling to the bottom of the boat with deep regret and abhorrence; 3) determination to stop the movements away from intimacy with God; and 4) avoidance of nongodly sorrow. (Note: godly sorrow leads to a restoration of relationship and lightness of being. Nongodly sorrow can lead to self-condemnation, despair, pity, and self-indulgence.)

---

[4] Dallas Willard, *Living in Christ's Presence: Final Words on Heaven and the Kingdom of God* (Downers Grove, IL: InterVarsity Press, 2014), 133.

Place an empty chair near you so that if a person were in that chair, they would be facing you, close enough to reach out and touch your knee.

Now imagine God is sitting in the chair. Read aloud the descriptions on page 24 of a person who is becoming a "child of light." Then confess to God where you are in terms of this being a description of you. If these are good descriptions of your current level of intimacy with God, wonderful; it is a cause for celebration. If they sound more like aspirational statements than descriptions of present reality, then turn the time into a confession.

SCRIPTURE FOR REFLECTION

Here are some passages to help you reflect on coming clean with God.

Since you have been raised to new life with Christ, set your sights on the realities of heaven, where Christ sits in the place of honor at God's right hand. Think about the things of heaven, not the things of earth. For you died to this life, and your real life is hidden with Christ in God. And when Christ, who is your life, is revealed to the whole world, you will share in all his glory.

So put to death the sinful, earthly things lurking within you. Have nothing to do with sexual immorality, impurity, lust, and evil desires. Don't be greedy, for a greedy person is an idolater, worshiping the things of this world. Because of these sins, the anger of God is coming. You used to do these things when your life was still part of this world. But now is the time to get rid of anger, rage, malicious behavior, slander, and dirty language. Don't lie to each other, for you have stripped off your old sinful nature and all its wicked deeds. Put on your new nature, and be renewed as you learn to know your Creator and become like him. In this new life, it doesn't matter if you are a Jew or a Gentile, circumcised or uncircumcised, barbaric, uncivilized, slave, or free. Christ is all that matters, and he lives in all of us.

Since God chose you to be the holy people he loves,
you must clothe yourselves with tenderhearted mercy,
kindness, humility, gentleness, and patience. Make
allowance for each other's faults, and forgive anyone
who offends you. Remember, the Lord forgave you, so
you must forgive others. Above all, clothe yourselves
with love, which binds us all together in perfect
harmony. And let the peace that comes from Christ
rule in your hearts. For as members of one body you
are called to live in peace. And always be thankful.

Let the message about Christ, in all its richness, fill
your lives. Teach and counsel each other with all the
wisdom he gives. Sing psalms and hymns and spiritual
songs to God with thankful hearts. And whatever you
do or say, do it as a representative of the Lord Jesus,
giving thanks through him to God the Father.

COLOSSIANS 3:1-17, NLT

Have mercy on me, O God,
  because of your unfailing love.
Because of your great compassion,
  blot out the stain of my sins.
Wash me clean from my guilt.
  Purify me from my sin.
For I recognize my rebellion;
  it haunts me day and night.
Against you, and you alone, have I sinned;
  I have done what is evil in your sight.
You will be proved right in what you say,

and your judgment against me is just.
For I was born a sinner—
    yes, from the moment my mother conceived me.
But you desire honesty from the womb,
    teaching me wisdom even there.

Purify me from my sins, and I will be clean;
    wash me, and I will be whiter than snow.
Oh, give me back my joy again;
    you have broken me—
    now let me rejoice.
Don't keep looking at my sins.
    Remove the stain of my guilt.
Create in me a clean heart, O God.
    Renew a loyal spirit within me.
Do not banish me from your presence,
    and don't take your Holy Spirit from me.

Restore to me the joy of your salvation,
    and make me willing to obey you.
Then I will teach your ways to rebels,
    and they will return to you.
Forgive me for shedding blood, O God who saves;
    then I will joyfully sing of your forgiveness.
Unseal my lips, O Lord,
    that my mouth may praise you.

You do not desire a sacrifice, or I would offer one.
    You do not want a burnt offering.

The sacrifice you desire is a broken spirit.
> You will not reject a broken and repentant heart,
>> O God.

Look with favor on Zion and help her;
> rebuild the walls of Jerusalem.

Then you will be pleased with sacrifices offered in the
>> right spirit—
> with burnt offerings and whole burnt offerings.
> Then bulls will again be sacrificed on your altar.

PSALM 51, NLT

Session 4

ILLUMINATION

WELCOME

Welcome to session 4 of the *Eternity Is Now in Session DVD Experience*. Each of the five sessions in this study is designed to be completed in 60 to 90 minutes, with additional activities that you can do at home.

This session accompanies chapter 6 of the *Eternity Is Now in Session* book (pages 125–145). Watch the video, discuss the questions, and complete the key activity as a group as time allows.

VIDEO NOTES

As you watch the video, use the space below to take notes. We've included some key points to get you started.

Jesus' most famous pop quiz has just one question on it: "Who do you say that I am?"

Caesarea Philippi was on the northernmost border of Israel. In ancient times so much water gushed out, they couldn't measure the depth of the pool. In the ancient world where water was sacred, this became a center for religious shrines.

Apparently, back at the beginning of their relationship, Jesus didn't say, "Believe the right things about me and you can be my disciples." He said, "Follow me, and you'll be my disciples." The idea that first you believe the right things about Jesus did not come from Jesus.

> Jesus replied, "Blessed are you, Simon son of Jonah, for this was not revealed to you by flesh and blood, but by my Father in heaven. And I tell you that you are Peter, and on this rock I will build my church, and the gates of Hades will not overcome it."
>
> MATTHEW 16:17-18

Jesus' main vehicle on earth is going to be the church. Jesus' main problem on earth is going to be the church. You can get the right answers and still become the wrong person.

> If anyone would come after me, he must deny himself and take up his cross and follow me. For whoever wants to save his life will lose it, but whoever loses his life for me will find it.
>
> MATTHEW 16:24-25

Jesus doesn't want people whose main goal and identity is that they give right religious answers. Those are the people who are going to kill him. He doesn't want answer givers; he wants life givers.

Arise, shine, for your light has come,
and the glory of the LORD rises upon you.

ISAIAH 60:1

DISCUSSION QUESTIONS

1. Why had Jesus not already told the disciples the right answer for the "pop quiz"? Why did he choose Caesarea Philippi as the backdrop for this teaching?

2. How would you describe, in practical, day-to-day terms, what it is like to be "blessed" by being in a living relationship with "Christ, the son of the God who is alive"?

3. What does it mean to pick up your cross and follow Jesus? How does that change your identity as a Christ-follower?

4. Are you in school to become a "child of light"? Why or why not? What is your curriculum like?

5. Over the past couple of weeks, what were your most spiritually high and spiritually low moments? When have you felt affirmed by God? When have you felt corrected?

KEY ASSESSMENT: WHO AM I—WHAT IS MY TRUEST IDENTITY?

In this teaching, Jesus focuses on identity, first his own and then that of Peter. He does this against the backdrop of Caesarea Philippi and its display of a massive wall of idols—nonliving gods. He offers this spiritual life lesson near a deep spring of water that is a primary source of the Jordan River—the place where John the Baptist offered baptism into a new identity. With baptism, there is a rethinking and a letting go of false sources of security and intimacy.

ASSESSMENT 1: IDOL IDENTIFICATION QUOTIENT

What is your IIQ (Idol Identification Quotient)? Take a moment to rate yourself on some of the common idols that John lists. As Tim Keller has said, an idol is a good thing that only becomes a bad thing if we try to make it into the ultimate thing.[5] To what extent is each of the following a potential substitute for your full identity being an intimate friend to Jesus?

	Not a Problem "with Jesus"	Absolutely a Major Idol
1. Money	1——2——3——4——5——6——7——8——9——10	
2. Sex	1——2——3——4——5——6——7——8——9——10	
3. Power	1——2——3——4——5——6——7——8——9——10	
4. Position	1——2——3——4——5——6——7——8——9——10	
5. Relationship	1——2——3——4——5——6——7——8——9——10	
6. [You Name It]	1——2——3——4——5——6——7——8——9——10	

[5] Timothy Keller, *Counterfeit Gods: The Empty Promises of Money, Sex, and Power, and the Only Hope That Matters* (New York: Penguin Books, 2016).

ASSESSMENT 2: TRUE IDENTITY

What does intimacy with Jesus look like? It means both freedom from the idols that would otherwise demand intimacy with our hearts, and it means honesty about our true identity with Jesus. Continuing with raw honesty in assessing your IIQ, use the following scales to rate your identity as a stranger, acquaintance, admirer, follower, or intimate friend of Jesus.

	No Way This Describes Our Relationship	This Is a Good Word for Where We Are
1. Stranger	1——2——3——4——5——6——7——8——9——10	
2. Acquaintance	1——2——3——4——5——6——7——8——9——10	
3. Admirer	1——2——3——4——5——6——7——8——9——10	
4. Follower	1——2——3——4——5——6——7——8——9——10	
5. Intimate Friend	1——2——3——4——5——6——7——8——9——10	
6. [You Name It]	1——2——3——4——5——6——7——8——9——10	

To the extent that you are comfortable, share your results and your feelings about those results with others in the group. Consider the following questions individually and as a group:

- Are you happy with your results?
- In what areas can you grow in your relationship with Jesus?
- In what ways can the group support you in your growing relationship with Jesus?

You may also want to consider this question as a group: What is your old name and what would you like your new name to be? See Revelation 2:17 (on page 55).

HOMEWORK: RECOGNIZE AND RESPOND

Before the next session, read chapter 7, "Union" (pages 147–173), in the *Eternity Is Now in Session* book. Consider also completing the following activities:

1. DAILY SCRIPTURE STUDY ON IDENTITY

God created each of us with unique characteristics and purpose and to walk with him in an interactive, transforming friendship. We discover both our individual identity (the one no one else has) and our identity that we share with others (friends of Jesus). Consider a slow reading of each of the following Bible verses this week to understand more about our identity in Christ and how to not lose sight of who we are destined to be.

- Sunday: 1 John 3:1-2 (children of God); Revelation 2:17 (given a new name)
- Monday: Genesis 1:27 (created in the image of God)
- Tuesday: John 1:12 (a child of God)
- Wednesday: Romans 6:6 (no longer a slave to sin)
- Thursday: 1 Corinthians 6:19-20 (temple of the Holy Spirit)
- Friday: Ephesians 1:5 (adopted into God's family)
- Saturday: 1 Peter 2:9 (God's special possession, called into the light)

2. CHILD OF LIGHT EXERCISE REVISITED

How is it going on your journey into a new identity? Take a few minutes and rate yourself again on how each of the components of you are progressing in their own transfiguration. Again, we'll use what Dallas Willard had to say about a person becoming a "child of light":

- *Thoughts*: Children of light think constantly about God, dwelling upon his greatness and loveliness.
- *Feelings*: Love is the dominant emotion of children of light.
- *Will (spirit, heart)*: They are habitually devoted to doing what is good and right. The will is habitually attuned to surrender and obey.
- *Body*: Their body is constantly poised to do what is right and good.
- *Social Relations*: Children of light are completely transparent in their relations with others.
- *Soul*: All of the above is not just at the surface; these things are deep and effortless.

SCRIPTURE FOR REFLECTION

Imitate God, therefore, in everything you do, because you are his dear children. Live a life filled with love, following the example of Christ. He loved us and offered himself as a sacrifice for us, a pleasing aroma to God.

Let there be no sexual immorality, impurity, or greed among you. Such sins have no place among God's people. Obscene stories, foolish talk, and coarse jokes—these are not for you. Instead, let there be thankfulness to God. You can be sure that no immoral, impure, or greedy person will inherit the Kingdom of Christ and of God. For a greedy person is an idolater, worshiping the things of this world.

Don't be fooled by those who try to excuse these sins, for the anger of God will fall on all who disobey him. Don't participate in the things these people do. For once you were full of darkness, but now you have light from the Lord. So live as people of light! For this light within you produces only what is good and right and true.

Carefully determine what pleases the Lord. Take no part in the worthless deeds of evil and darkness; instead, expose them. It is shameful even to talk about the things that ungodly people do in secret. But their evil intentions will be exposed when the light shines on them, for the light makes everything visible. This is why it is said,

"Awake, O sleeper,
 rise up from the dead,
 and Christ will give you light."
EPHESIANS 5:1-14, NLT

Anyone with ears to hear must listen to the Spirit
and understand what he is saying to the churches.
To everyone who is victorious I will give some of the
manna that has been hidden away in heaven. And I
will give to each one a white stone, and on the stone
will be engraved a new name that no one understands
except the one who receives it.
REVELATION 2:17, NLT

Session 5

UNION

WELCOME

Welcome to the final session of the *Eternity Is Now in Session DVD Experience*. Each of the five sessions in this study is designed to be completed in 60 to 90 minutes, with additional activities that you can do at home.

This session accompanies chapter 7 of the *Eternity Is Now in Session* book (pages 147–173). Watch the video, discuss the questions, and complete the key activity as a group as time allows.

VIDEO NOTES

As you watch the video, use the space below to take notes. We've included some key points to get you started.

Jesus offers you a picture and an invitation: I am the vine, you are the branches. Abide in me.

Living in connection with God is not about where; it's about how.

> I am the vine, you are the branches. Those
> who abide in me and I in them bear much fruit,
> because apart from me you can do nothing.
>
> JOHN 15:5, NRSV

If you understand the picture, if you accept the invitation, Jesus says you can have an intimate relationship of love with God.

What is abiding? When you abide, you make a home in a place, you linger there, and your inner person—your spirit—gets shaped by your abode. You can abide in fear. You can abide in ambition. You can abide in anger. You can abide in lust. Or you can abide in God. God wants to make your heart his home. God wants to make his heart your home.

The branch's job is not to produce fruit. The branch's job is to learn to continually receive life from the vine. The fruit is a by-product of abiding.

We will never produce the right fruit by trying to produce the right fruit. It is the inside of the branch that must change. The automatic flow of thoughts and desires and intentions must change from being ego centered and conflicted and greedy and fearful, to confident and grateful and humble and joyful and always ready to love.

Abide in me as I abide in you. Just as the branch
cannot bear fruit by itself unless it abides in the
vine, neither can you unless you abide in me.

JOHN 15:4, NRSV

Your job is not to try to generate more God-pleasing actions by
greater willpower. Your job is to abide.

DISCUSSION QUESTIONS

1. If the branch's job is not to produce fruit, what is the job description for a branch? How does John describe the "fruit" that branches are to produce? What must change for the "fruit of the Spirit," the very character of Christ, to be produced in your life?

2. What are your primary obstacles to abiding in God through the day as a branch that is connected to a vine? What are possible ways to overcome these obstacles?

3. How do spiritual disciplines help with living in friendship with Jesus? What spiritual disciplines have you tried? Which do you think would be most effective for you?

4. What does it mean that the thoughts are the roots of your spirit? How do your thoughts affect your life on the vine?

5. How do you usually react when you mess up? As a branch on the vine, how should you react? What would change if you consistently reacted this way?

KEY ASSESSMENT: THE ABC'S OF THOUGHT

Take a look at the following illustration. On the table is a pool cue that is labeled A. The pool cue is about to strike a ball (labeled B) that will in turn strike a second ball (C), and if the rules of physics are properly applied, C will drop into the pocket of the table—a successful shot.

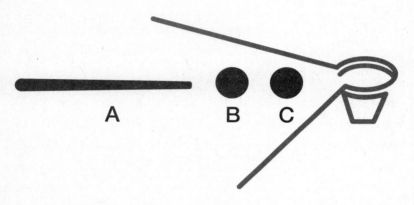

This pool diagram represents the role your thoughts play in other aspects of your life—particularly your emotions. The pool cue represents an event from your day—any event. Let's say you are at work, and your boss says, "I would like to see you later today." This brief contact with your boss is an A, which stands for "activating event."

B in this scenario represents your "immediate belief"—that is, the first thought or thoughts that pass through your mind. If your thought is, *Oh, no! I'm going to be fired*, you will probably have a pretty bad day, with emotions (that's the C, "emotional consequence") of anxiety and dread.

But on the other hand, if your first thoughts are *This is*

wonderful; I'm finally going to get that promotion!, then your emotions will be drastically different: excited anticipation.

It is important to note that the pool cue (activating event) did not change. In both cases it was an ambiguous encounter with your boss, who said, "I want to see you later today." What changed? The thoughts that played in your head like CDs in a jukebox (or a random iTunes shuffle of your top 25 playlist). The radically different thoughts produced radically different emotions.

Let's look at one more "A-B-C" example. Imagine you are driving in your car. A light you were hoping to catch while still green turns red. That's A, the "activating event." The "emotional consequence" (C) of the red light will not be caused by the light but by the thoughts and beliefs (B) that flash through your mind. If you think, *Oh great! I bet I'll catch every one now. I'll be late for my hair appointment and will probably miss it*, that type of B will cause some pretty unpleasant C.

But if the light changes (A) and you think (B), *This is great! I needed a sixty-second vacation. I'll take three or four deep, slow breaths and relax*, well, your C will be very different: gratitude for the mini-vacation.

By changing our thoughts (and it is quite possible to do so), we can change more than our emotions; we can participate in the process of authentic spiritual transformation. To a large extent, our thoughts are under our control. We can set out to change them, and the results can be not only different emotional consequences but also changes in our will, behavior, and social interactions.

EXERCISE

Take a few minutes to unplug and take a few deep and slow breaths. Then ask yourself the question, *What is the most common thought I have about myself?* Whether that thought is good, bad, or neutral, breathe it in and out for a while. Then note how you are feeling.

Now, breathe this thought for a while: *I am an eternal spiritual being in whom God dwells and delights.* Breathe that thought for a while as you allow yourself to sink into the truth that your very existence is in an ocean of divine love. Then note again: How are you feeling? What changed? Only the primary thought in your mind.

HOMEWORK: RECOGNIZE AND RESPOND

This is the final session of the *Eternity Is Now in Session* curriculum, but the experience needn't end here. These are some activities you can complete in the next week:

1. DAILY SCRIPTURE STUDY ON UNION AS A *LECTIO DIVINA* PRAYER

Lectio divina is a slow, contemplative way of praying the Scriptures that enables the Word of God to become a means of union with God. It is one classic way of allowing the Word and presence of Christ to penetrate to the center of our being and begin a process of transforming us from the inside out.

There are four movements contained within this method of praying Scripture. The first movement is called "reading" or "listening." The practice of *lectio divina* begins with cultivating the ability to listen deeply, to hear "with the ear of our hearts," as St. Benedict describes in the prologue of his Rule. It is a way of being more sensitive to the still, small voice of God (see 1 Kings 19:12), the "faint murmuring sound" that is God's word for us, his voice touching our hearts.

The reading or listening step in *lectio divina* is very different from the speed reading you may be used to applying to magazines or novels. *Lectio* is reverential listening, listening in a spirit both of silence and of awe. In *lectio* we read slowly and attentively, gently listening to hear a word or phrase that is God's communication for us this day.

The second phase of *lectio* is meditation. Once through "listening," if we have found a word, passage, or image in the Scripture that speaks to us in a personal way, we must take it in and ruminate on it. We ponder it in our hearts. We do this by gently repeating a key word or phrase, allowing it to interact with our thoughts, hopes, memories, and desires. Through this phase we allow the word from God to become his word *for us*, a word that touches us at our deepest levels.

The third step is prayer: prayer understood both as dialogue with God (that is, as loving conversation with the one who has invited us into his embrace) and as consecration (that is, as the priestly offering to God of parts of ourselves that we have not previously believed God wants). Here we allow the word that we have taken in and on which we are pondering to touch and change our deepest selves.

The final step is to rest in the presence of the one who has used his Word as a means of inviting us to accept his transforming embrace. It is the phase called "contemplation," where there are moments when words are unnecessary. Contemplation is wordless, quiet rest in the presence of the one who loves us.

In the practice of *lectio divina*, you will choose a text of Scripture that you wish to pray. Let's start with Psalm 1 (see page 72).

Here is what to do next:

- Place yourself in a comfortable position and allow yourself to become silent.
- *Read/Listen*: Turn to the text and read it slowly, gently. Savor each portion of the reading, constantly listening for the "still, small voice" of a word or phrase that somehow says, "I am for you today."

- *Meditate*: Next, take the word or phrase into yourself. Memorize it and slowly repeat it to yourself, allowing it to interact with your inner world of concerns, memories, and ideas. Do not be afraid of distractions. Memories or thoughts are simply parts of you. Don't try to chase them away; just return to the word you are pondering.
- *Converse*: Then, speak to God. Whether you use words, ideas, images, or all three is not important. Interact with God as you would with one who you know loves and accepts you. Give to God what you have discovered in yourself during your experience.
- *Rest*: Finally, simply rest in God's embrace. Enjoy his presence. And when he invites you to return to your pondering of his Word or to your inner dialogue with him, do so. Rejoice in the knowledge that God is with you in both words and silence.

You've started with Psalm 1. Sometime this week, try this practice again with John 15:4-15 and Philippians 4:8-9 and then with another passage of your choosing.

2. LIVING PLUGGED IN
Make a game out of keeping plugged into God this week, remaining in his presence. Try some of these, or your own, ideas:

- Memorize either the Twenty-third Psalm or the Lord's Prayer. Before getting out of bed each morning, breathe the verses as a prayer.

- Set a clock or timer (such as your smartphone or Fitbit) to remind you—morning, noon, and evening—to stop and pray.
- During one of those pauses, breathe the Nicene Creed.
- During another pause, allow love for others to flow out into intercession.
- Take time to step into a passage of Scripture using *lectio divina.*
- When you are in conversation and see the eyes of the person you are with, be reminded that Christ lives inside that person.
- Every time you glance at a watch, clock, or phone to check the time, be prompted to pray internally, *Lord, Jesus Christ, have mercy on me.*
- Take the time to admire the beauty of a plant, tree, or flower and then admire the Designer.
- Leave an empty chair at each meal as a reminder that you are not alone.
- Leave an empty chair by your computer as both a reminder and accountability check that you are not alone.
- Perform an act of service for another person (in secret, if possible) as an act of love for God.
- End the day with the examen (for a refresher, see page 33). Reflect on the times when you felt most close to and most distant from God.

SCRIPTURE FOR REFLECTION

Remain in me, and I will remain in you. For a branch
cannot produce fruit if it is severed from the vine, and
you cannot be fruitful unless you remain in me.

Yes, I am the vine; you are the branches. Those who
remain in me, and I in them, will produce much fruit.
For apart from me you can do nothing. Anyone who
does not remain in me is thrown away like a useless
branch and withers. Such branches are gathered into
a pile to be burned. But if you remain in me and my
words remain in you, you may ask for anything you
want, and it will be granted! When you produce much
fruit, you are my true disciples. This brings great glory
to my Father.

I have loved you even as the Father has loved
me. Remain in my love. When you obey my
commandments, you remain in my love, just as I obey
my Father's commandments and remain in his love.
I have told you these things so that you will be filled
with my joy. Yes, your joy will overflow! This is my
commandment: Love each other in the same way I have
loved you. There is no greater love than to lay down
one's life for one's friends. You are my friends if you do
what I command. I no longer call you slaves, because
a master doesn't confide in his slaves. Now you are my
friends, since I have told you everything the Father
told me.

JOHN 15:4-15, NLT

Oh, the joys of those who do not
   follow the advice of the wicked,
   or stand around with sinners,
   or join in with mockers.
But they delight in the law of the LORD,
   meditating on it day and night.
They are like trees planted along the riverbank,
   bearing fruit each season.
Their leaves never wither,
   and they prosper in all they do.

But not the wicked!
   They are like worthless chaff, scattered by the wind.
They will be condemned at the time of judgment.
   Sinners will have no place among the godly.
For the LORD watches over the path of the godly,
   but the path of the wicked leads to destruction.

PSALM 1, NLT

ABOUT THE AUTHORS

John Ortberg is an author, a speaker, and the senior pastor of Menlo Church in the San Francisco Bay Area. A consistent theme of John's teaching is how to follow a Jesus way of life—that is, how faith in Christ can affect our everyday lives with God. His books include *All the Places to Go . . . How Will You Know?*; *Soul Keeping*; *Who Is This Man?*; *The Life You've Always Wanted*; *Faith and Doubt*; and *If You Want to Walk on Water, You've Got to Get Out of the Boat*. John teaches around the world at conferences and churches.

Born and raised in Rockford, Illinois, John graduated from Wheaton College. He holds a master's of divinity and a doctorate in clinical psychology from Fuller Seminary, and he did postgraduate work at the University of Aberdeen, Scotland.

John is a member of the board of trustees at Fuller Seminary, where he has also served as an adjunct faculty member. He is on the board of the Dallas Willard Center for Christian Spiritual Formation and has served in the past on the board of Christianity Today International.

Now that their children are grown, John and his wife, Nancy, enjoy surfing in the Pacific to help care for their souls. He can be followed on Twitter @johnortberg.

Gary W. Moon (PhD, Fuller Theological Seminary) is director of the Martin Family Institute and the Dallas Willard Center for Christian Spiritual Formation at Westmont College in Santa Barbara, California. He is also codirector of Fuller's doctor of ministry degree program in spiritual direction, which blends ancient Christian spirituality, Ignatian spirituality, and spiritual formation insights from Dallas Willard. He served as distinguished professor of psychology and Christian spirituality at Richmont Graduate University, editor in chief for the journal *Conversations*, and the director of the Renovaré International Institute for Christian Spiritual Formation. His books include *Apprenticeship with Jesus* and *Falling for God*.

WANT TO LEARN MORE ABOUT

THE DOORS GOD HAS

PROVIDED FOR YOU?

All the Places to Go
Overcome uncertainty and
learn to live an open-door life.

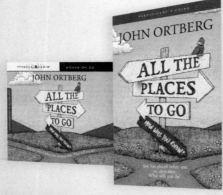

**All the Places
to Go**
AUDIO CD
An audio version
to listen anywhere.

**All the Places
to Go**
PARTICIPANT'S GUIDE
Great for small
group and personal
Bible study.

**All the Places
to Go**
DVD CURRICULUM
DVD companion to
the participant's
guide with additional
in-depth teaching
from John Ortberg.

**What Is God's
Will for My Life?**
BOOKLET
Helps you
discover God's
plan for your life.

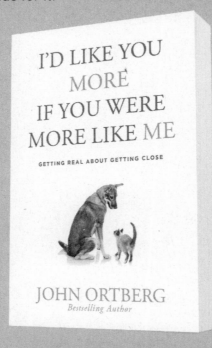

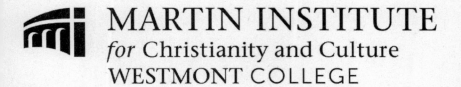

MARTIN INSTITUTE
for Christianity and Culture
WESTMONT COLLEGE

The Martin Institute for Christianity and Culture is dedicated to placing an enduring emphasis on spiritual formation with a particular focus on the path of authentic transformation as an interactive, loving relationship with Jesus Christ. As part of that quest, we hope to honor the legacy of Dallas Willard while placing his work in the context of other thought and praxis leaders who have developed methods for authentic Christian formation that have stood the test of time.

The Goals:

The goals of the Martin Institute for Christianity and Culture are to 1) support a new generation of thought leaders in the area of Christian spiritual formation and 2) help establish this discipline as a domain of public knowledge that is open to research and pedagogy of the highest order.

The Centers:

Dallas Willard Research Center: Supports and engages in Christian spiritual formation research and writing efforts through 1) maintaining and offering access to the books and papers of Dallas Willard's personal library, including online availability for many of these resources; 2) a senior fellows program; 3) annual book and research awards programs; and 4) providing faculty research retreats.

Conversatio Divina: A Center for Spiritual Renewal: Creates and offers resources for both "pilgrims" and "guides." Specific activities include 1) academic course development for pastors, church leaders, spiritual directors, and mental health professionals; 2) development of small group curriculum projects in the area of spiritual formation; 3) a variety of writing efforts; and 4) continuing education and retreat offerings for ministry leaders.

Westmont Center for Spiritual Formation: Offers spiritual formation opportunities for the Westmont community through providing a retreat space and programming along with partnerships across campus. Specific offerings include small group development, residence-life-based spiritual formation coordinators, and support for Augustinian Scholars and chapel programs.

For more information, visit www.dallaswillardcenter.com.

CP1383